HYMNS AND POEMS

Hymns

and

Poems

BY

A. L. O. E.

(Charlotte Maria Tucker)

AUTHOR OF "THE ROBBER'S CAVE" AND "THE MINE."

CURIOSMITH

MINNEAPOLIS

Published by Curiosmith.
Minneapolis, Minnesota.
Internet: curiosmith.com.

Previously published by T. NELSON & SONS in 1868.

Supplementary content, book layout, and cover design:
Copyright © 2016 Charles J. Doe

ISBN 9781941281642

CONTENTS

——○◦✤◦○——

POEMS

PREFACE

If there be any distinctive peculiarity in this little volume, it is one that would naturally expose it to literary censure; the verses are very unequal, some of the hymns are avowedly written for the very poor. To admit rhymes for ragged children, needlewomen, and paupers into a book of sacred song, may—in the opinion of some critics—deprive it of all claim to the name of poetry. Yet I venture to hope that those who love to labor in God's vineyard, will not be sorry to bear to their poorer brethren verses intended to meet their peculiar trials, and cheer them under their peculiar sorrows; while the subjects of many of the hymns are such as are of equal interest to the prince as to the peasant. Humbly I commend my little work to Him whose blessing can alone make it useful in strengthening the tempted, in cheering the sad, or in lifting up the hearts of the happy in joyful adoration and praise.

A. L. O. E.

HYMNS.

THE WILLING SACRIFICE

The precious blood of Christ my Lord,
    The Saviour all-divine,
Was shed to cleanse men's souls from guilt;
    That blood has flowed for mine!
But what return can sinners make
    For love so great, so free?
All is too little, oh! my God,
    To sacrifice to Thee.

If all that I possessed on earth,
    Before thy feet were laid,
Light as the dust the gift would prove
    In heaven's balance weighed.
The costly treasures of the skies
    Thou didst resign for me;
All is too little, oh! my God,
    To sacrifice to Thee.

But Thou wilt not disdain a heart
    That would Thy word obey,
That loves to own the mighty debt
    It never hopes to pay.
For were each hair upon my head
    A separate life to be,[1]
All were too little, oh! my God,
    To sacrifice to Thee.

---

1 The expression used by one who now rests in Christ.

THE RESURRECTION

The Summer blossoms fast decay
 Beneath the Autumn's chilling breath,
And man is passing thus away,
 Touched by the silent hand of Death.
Still fading—falling—day by day
 The withered petals strew the plain,
They never more shall deck the spray—
 But man shall rise again!

Behold the bare and leafless tree
 Blushes in spring to beauty bright;
Where the dark root was buried—see
 The eager floweret springs to light!
The sun his gentle influence shed
 To break cold winter's icy chain—
So God shall wake us from the dead,
 We all shall rise again!

As beauteous day succeeds to night,
 So glory dawns upon the grave—
Praise to the Sun of life and light,
 Who lived to bless, and died to save!
We calmly gaze on life's dark close,
 The tomb shall not our forms retain—
E'en as our God and Saviour rose
 His own shall rise again!

HYMN FOR THE COMMUNION

I do not dare, O holy Lord,
    Approach Thy sacred shrine
Trusting in mine own righteousness,
    For nought but sins are mine,
But in the merits of Thy Son,
    The Saviour all-divine.

Unworthy as I own I am
    Christ's feast of love to share,
In His name hear my humble cry,
    For His sake grant my prayer,
And let Thy mercy cleanse my soul,
    And shed Thy Spirit there!

Oh, make me one with my dear Lord
    In His appointed rite,
A branch of the Eternal Vine
    Not fruitless in His sight;
His own on earth, His own in heaven
    Through ages infinite!

THE BEACON

When shades of night around him close,
    The lighthouse guard has charge to keep,
And trim the beacon-fire, which glows
    Like a red star above the deep.
        Still calm and bright
        Must shine that light
    That guides the seaman on his way,
        Till morning gleam
        And lighthouse beam
    Fade in the rosy blush of day.

Like charge is to the Christian given
    In grief or joy, in storm or strife,
To glorify the God of heaven
    Both by his lips and by his life.
        Still pure and bright
        Must shine his light,
    And shed around a holy ray,
        A flame of love
        Lit from above,
    And shining on to perfect day.

Pride, discontent, mistrustful fear,
    Too oft, alas! the beacon hide;
The sinner must be humbled here
    That Jesus may be glorified.
        So pure and bright
        Shall shine his light,
    To other hearts a beam convey,
        A flame of love
        Lit from above,
    Still shining on to perfect day.

Lord, feed our lamps with heavenly grace,
    And let them to Thy glory shine,

Nor let our weakness e'er disgrace
   The holy faith which seals us Thine!
      Then pure and bright
      Shall shine our light,
   Our heavenly Father's grace display,
      A flame of love
      Lit from above,
   Still shining on to perfect day!

THE BLOSSOMING ROD

An angel of comfort from heaven sped—
    All nature brightened as he drew near
Where a poor man toiled in his lowly shed
And thanked the Lord for his scanty bread;
    The angel breathed in the Christian's ear,
"Thy God beholds, and will not forget;
    Have patience—the rod will blossom yet!"

He spread his pinions, then paused again
    Where prayer from a sick man's couch was heard;
In weary weakness, in restless pain,
For tedious months had the sufferer lain,
    But his pale face beamed at the whispered word:
"Thy God beholds, and will not forget;
    Have patience—the rod will blossom yet!"

Then the angel flew where a mother prayed
    For a son on a course of evil bent;
She wept—half trustful and half afraid,
Beseeching Him who alone could aid;
    And to her was the message of comfort sent—
"Thy God beholds, and will not forget;
    Have patience—the rod will blossom yet!"

With cares depressed, and with trials worn,
    A persecuted believer knelt;
With drooping heart she had meekly borne
The unkind taunt and the look of scorn,
    Till the angel's smile was like sunshine felt.
"Thy God beholds, and will not forget;
    Have patience—the rod will blossom yet!"

Then the seraph hovered where death had been,
    In its little coffin an infant lay;

The parents wept, but a calm serene
Stole over their souls, as a hand unseen
    Gently wiped the trickling tears away.
"Your God beholds, and will not forget;
Your bud shall blossom in glory yet!"

Happy such to whom griefs come not in vain,
    Though afflictions bow, or the world contemn,
Thrice blest in sorrow, thrice blest in pain,
Reproach is honour, and loss is gain,
    For the angel of peace shall visit them—
Their God beholds, and will not forget;
Their rod shall blossom in glory yet!

HYMN FOR THE PENITENT CONVICT

I dare not raise my guilty eye
    The gaze of man to meet,
A helpless sentenced wretch I lie,
    Lord Jesus! at Thy feet.
Too justly scorned by all beside,
    I trembling come to Thee;
If Thou for *chief of sinners* died,
    Is there not hope for me?

The dying thief in torments hung
    While sinners scoffed around;
With feeble breath and faltering tongue
    He mercy sought—and found.
There flowed before his eyesight dim
    The blood which made him free;
If Jesus heard and pitied him
    Is there not hope for me?

The weeping prodigal returned
    His father's house to seek;
His supplication was not spurned—
    Love still could welcome speak.
Like him, in grief and penitence,
    To mercy's door I flee,
O Father, wilt thou spurn me thence;
    Is there not hope for me?

Yes, there is hope! while He, once crowned
    With thorns, now pleads in heaven,
Rejoices o'er the lost one found,
    The wanderer forgiven;
To those who mourn and turn from sin
    He offers mercy free;
I feel another life begin—
    There yet is hope for me!

HYMN FOR THE BLIND

I cannot see the sunny gleam
   Which gladdens every eye but mine,
But I can feel the warming beam,
   And bless the God who made it shine.
O Lord, each murmuring thought control,
   Let no repining tear-drop fall,
Pour holy light upon my soul,
   That I may own Thy love in all!

I cannot see the flow'rets blow,
   All sparkling from the summer showers,
But I can breathe their sweet perfume,
   And bless the God who made the flowers.
O Lord, each murmuring thought control,
   Let no repining tear-drop fall,
Pour holy light upon my soul,
   That I may own Thy love in all!

I cannot see the pages where
   Thy holy will is written, Lord;
But I can seek Thy house of prayer,
   And humbly listen to Thy word,
Which bears my thoughts to that bright place
   Where I at Thy dear feet may fall,
Behold my Saviour face to face,
   And see and own His love in all!

THE HOUSE NOT MADE WITH HANDS

The stately mansion riseth beneath the builder's hand,
When our children sleep in dust that mansion still may stand;
But a nobler and more lasting dwelling to the saints is given,
In a house not made with hands, eternal in the Heaven.

The poor in spirit and the meek, the merciful and pure,
On them the Saviour blessings breathed, for ever to endure;
Those persecuted for His sake, from friends or kindred driven,
Share a house not made with hands, eternal in the Heaven.

And those who deeply mourn their sins shall find there yet is room,
For such the Lord endured the cross, descended to the tomb;
He ready stands to welcome those whose contrite hearts are riven,
To a house not made with hands, eternal in the Heaven.

What matter, then, how lowly be the roof above our head,
What matter then how soon the stranger o'er our graves may tread,
If we are pressing on with hearts renewed and sins forgiven,
To a house not made with hands, eternal in the Heaven!

SEXTON'S HYMN

I've laid the earth above the child
   Whose life was but a summer's day;
I knew that God, in mercy mild,
   Had called his happy soul away.
     Then wherefore weep
     O'er those who sleep?
Their precious dust the Lord will keep,
     Till He appear
     In glory here,
The harvest of the earth to reap.

I've laid the earth above the youth
   Whose early days to God were given,
Whose end bore witness to this truth,
   None die too soon who live for Heaven!
     Then wherefore weep
     O'er those who sleep?
Their precious dust the Lord will keep,
     Till He appear
     In glory here,
The harvest of the earth to reap.

I've laid the earth o'er reverend age,
   Whose hoary hairs were glory's crown,
The saint had closed his pilgrimage,
   And gently laid life's burden down.
     Then wherefore weep
     O'er those who sleep?
Their precious dust the Lord will keep,
     Till He appear
     In glory here,
The harvest of the earth to reap.

And soon the earth will close o'er me,

Yet mourn I not my life's decline,
Lord! pardoned—ransomed—saved by Thee,
Living or dying—I am Thine!
Oh! wherefore sigh
For those who die
In Christ? the forms that mouldering lie
Shall burst the sod
To meet their God,
And mount with seraph wings on high!

THE SECOND ADVENT

Now in the East Hope's trembling light
 Proclaims a brighter dawning,
Though woe endureth for a night,
 Joy cometh in the morning.

For many weary ages past
 Hath sin's dark night prevailing,
A gloom o'er all the nations cast,
 Whence rose the sound of wailing.
The idol-gods have many a shrine
 Where, bound in chains of error,
Myriads shut out from light divine
 Crouch down in shame and terror.
But in the East Hope's rosy light
 Proclaims a brighter dawning;
Though woe endureth for a night,
 Joy cometh in the morning.

Pleasure has thrown her torches' glare
 Upon a world benighted,
And Science in the murky air
 Her glimmering tapers lighted;
Some joys, like fireflies, played and glanced
 To mock our vain pursuing,
And Folly's meteors wildly danced
 Above the gulf of ruin!
But in the East Hope's purer light
 Proclaims a brighter dawning;
Though woe endureth for a night,
 Joy cometh in the morning!

Like Cynthia from her silver car,
 The Church could darkness brighten;
Each high example, like a star,

Shone forth to cheer and lighten.
But I shall need nor star nor moon
In that clear day before me,
The Sun of Righteousness shall soon
Burst forth in cloudless glory!
Yes, in the East Hope's kindling light
Proclaims a brighter dawning;
Though woe endureth for a night,
Joy cometh in the morning!

HOPES THAT ABIDE

Earth's bright hopes must fade,
    Not those which grace hath given;
Joys were fleeting made,
    But not the joys of Heaven!
Stars that shine above,
    And flowers that cannot wither,
These are types of peace and love
    That shall abide for ever.

Who that seeks the skies
    Would mourn earth's pleasures blighted,
Weep o'er broken ties
    Soon to be re-united?
Blest e'en awhile to be
    In darkness and in sorrow,
Assured we soon the dawn shall see
    Of an eternal morrow!

SOLDIER'S HYMN

There is a sword of glittering sheen,—
    All unite to defend the right!
Its blade is bright and its edge is keen,
But the wound it gives is a wound unseen,—
    And who would flinch in the glorious fight!

There is a foe—a ruthless foe—
    Such unite to oppose the right;
In secret ambush he croucheth low,
And the blow he strikes is a deadly blow,—
    But flinch not we in the glorious fight!

There is a banner floating wide,—
    All unite to defend the right!
The blood of martyrs its folds has dyed,
When the best and bravest fought side by side,—
    Who would not flinch in the glorious fight!

There is a Leader exalted high,—
    All unite to defend the right!
Through Him His followers hosts defy,
Through Him they learn to do and to die,
    And scorn to flinch in the glorious fight!

There is a palm—a victor's palm,—
    All unite to defend the right!
'Twill be given in realms of peace and calm
To the steadfast spirit, the stalwart arm,
    That never flinched in the glorious fight.

Then shall lips touched with living flame
    In song unite, in the world of light;—
In our Leader's strength, in our Leader's name,
We fought—we struggled—we overcame,
    And victors stood in the glorious fight!

HYMN FOR NIGHT

After labour sweet is rest,
    Gently the wearied eyelids close;
As an infant sleeps on his mother's breast,
    The child of God may in peace repose.
Whether we sleep, or whether we wake,
We are His who gave His life for our sake.

He to whom darkness is as light,
    Tenderly guards his slumbering sheep;
The Shepherd watches His flock by night,
    The feeble lambs He will safely keep.
Whether we sleep, or whether we wake,
We are His who gave His life for our sake.

Death's night comes,—it may now be near,—
    Lord! if our faith be fixed on Thee,
Oh! how calm will that rest appear,
    Oh! how sweet will the waking be!
Whether we sleep, or whether we wake,
We are His who gave His life for our sake.

SONG OF JOY

The balmy Spring awakes the flowers
 That long had slept in Winter's night,
Her light green robe adorns the bowers,
 And all is beauty, all delight.
With joy I view earth's smiling frame,
And bless, O Lord, and bless Thy name!

Thou hast vouchsafed me buoyant health,
 A cheerful, light, and bounding heart;
Contentment—better far than wealth,
 And Hope—that rests when joys depart.
What gratitude such gifts should claim,—
For these, O Lord, I bless thy name!

Surrounded from my earliest days
 By those who loved—who love me still,
My grateful heart I humbly raise
 To Him, by whose Almighty will
To me earth's sweetest blessings came;
I praise and magnify His name!

But more than all I thank Thee, Lord,
 For sins through Thy dear blood forgiven,
The comforts of Thy precious Word,
 And hopes of endless bliss in Heaven;
Bought by Thy suffering and Thy shame,—
For these, O Lord, I bless Thy name!

Lord! should it be Thy sovereign will
 To blast my earthly happiness,
Yet give me grace to praise Thee still,
 With trembling lips Thy wisdom bless;
Crushed or exalted—still the same,
To bless, with fervour bless Thy name!

Should all life's pleasures disappear,
    Support me with Thy heavenly love,—
And when my course is ended here,
    Oh, raise my soul to bliss above,
With saints to magnify Thy fame,
And bless, for ever bless Thy name!

THE RETROSPECT

When on Zion's hill we rest
In the mansions of the blest,
What a strange and fleeting dream
All life's hopes and fears will seem?

What will all our pleasures here—
Titles—honours—then appear?
Like a bubble on the river,
Bright awhile—then lost for ever!

Things that now employ each thought,
Warmly wished for, fondly sought—
We may smile, and wonder much
Heirs of Heaven could stoop to such!

Will the petty wrongs of earth
Seem one moment's anger worth;
Or a friend's depart—the sorrow
Felt by those so soon to follow?

All that time bestowed will be
Lost in bright eternity;
Save the harvest Christian Love
Sowed on earth—to reap above!

THE SUPPLICANT

A helpless sinner in Thy sight,
    At mercy's threshold, Lord, I wait;
Inscribed in characters of light,
    Thy promise shines upon the gate.
        "Ask—ye shall receive;
           Seek—and ye shall find;
        Knock—and enter in, but leave
           All sins and doubts behind."

I *ask* Thy boundless grace to share,
    I *seek* for pardon through Thy blood,
I *knock* by earnest, fervent prayer,—
    Lord, hear and answer me for good!
        "Ask—ye shall receive;
           Seek—and ye shall find;
        Knock—and enter in, but leave
           All sins and doubts behind."

Yes; each mistrustful doubt of Thee,
    Each long-indulged, besetting sin,
Repented and renounced must be
    By those who dare to venture in.
        Then asking—we receive,
           And seeking—we shall find,
        Till, entering Heaven's gate, we leave
           Earth, sin, and death behind!

WEAVER'S HYMN

How swiftly flies man's mortal thread
   Within the mighty loom of Time;
What brilliant hues on some are shed,
   While some are stained with woe or crime!
But they bright webs are weaving,
Who, trusting and believing,
Through scenes of sorrow, scenes of joy,
   God's grace are still receiving.

'Tis thus the Christian we behold
   In sickness and in want resigned,
Because religion's thread of gold
   Is in his gloomy lot entwined.
A bright web he is weaving
When, trusting and believing,
He from a loving Father's hand
   Each trial is receiving.

Death soon will break our thread in twain,
   Time's busy loom itself must rest;
Nought but a winding-sheet remain
   Of all that mortals here possest.
Then every trial leaving,
No more o'er sorrows grieving,
How blest the Christian, from his Lord
   The crown of life receiving!

EMIGRANT'S HYMN

Father of Heaven, Thy guidance we implore
    Where'er Thy providence our steps may send;
With drooping hearts we leave our native shore,
    Do Thou be with us always—to the end!

Protect and guard us on the lonely sea,
    Though angry storms our flutt'ring canvas rend,
The anchor of our hope is fixed on Thee,
    Do Thou be with us always—to the end!

Prepare for us a home beyond the wave,
    Where we in honest toil our days may spend,
Till gently sinking to a peaceful grave;
    And be Thou with us always—to the end!

Oh! bless the dear ones whom we leave behind!
    Though severed now from parent—brother—friend—
In Thee the parted yet may union find,
    With them and us be always—to the end!

Nor time nor space can from Thy love divide;
    For ever near to bless and to defend,
Our lives—our all—we to Thy care confide,
    Be with us always—even to the end!

FISHERMEN'S HYMN

There were fishermen once by the blue Galilee,
    Whose lives were as toilsome and hard as our own,
They launched in the morning their boats in the sea,
    Their nets in the soft heaving waters were thrown.

A plentiful blessing rewarded their toil,
    Though all the night long they had laboured in vain,
Their vessels were filled with the glittering spoil,
    And slowly, deep-laden, they moved o'er the main.

'Twas the presence of Christ that a miracle wrought,
    The richly filled net was cast forth at His word,
And the draught far surpassing their hopes or their thought,
    Was the least of the blessings bestowed by the Lord.

Be with us, O Lord! when we launch forth alone,
    Be with us when toiling our bread to obtain,
Though Thy presence no more be by miracles known,
    Who labour in faith, will not labour in vain.

But we ask Thee for blessings more precious by far
    Than the depths of the earth or the ocean can yield,
Make us feel, like Thy Peter, what sinners we are,
    Make us know that, though sinners, our pardon is sealed.

Make us willing to quit all that keep us from Thee,
    Like the chosen disciples in ages long past,
Like them, throughout life, Thy true followers be,
    And anchor in Heaven's safe haven at last!

TEACHER'S HYMN

"Feed thou My lambs," the Saviour said
    To one whose spirit burned to prove
By toils endured, or life-blood shed,
    The strength of his devoted love.

"Feed thou My lambs;" oh! sacred trust
    E'en for a great apostle meet,
To raise the feeble from the dust,
    And guide them to the Saviour's feet.

"Feed thou My lambs." And ever thus
    His flock the heavenly Shepherd tends;
His mild command He breathes to us,
    And to our care His sheep commends.

"Feed thou My lambs;" despised on earth
    The friendless little one may be,
But who can tell the priceless worth
    Of one soul, Lord, redeemed by Thee!

May we pursue the blest employ
    Endowed with wisdom from above,
And count it privilege and joy
    To feed the lambs whom Thou dost love!

WORKMAN'S HYMN

Before the morning's toil begin,
    We thank Thee, Giver of all good,
For needful health and strength to win,
    By daily labour, daily food.

The seeing eye, the skilful hand,
    The powerful arm, are gifts from Thee;
Thou for our comfort all hast planned,
    Used to Thy glory all should be.

When Thou didst come to visit man,
    A lowly lot, O Lord, was Thine;
In poverty Thy life began,
    Shall we at poverty repine?

Thou who dost all our trials know,
    Thou who didst all our sorrows share,
The comforts of Thy grace bestow,
    And make us rich in faith and prayer.

Soon will the hours of toil be past,
    And calm repose at night be given;
So life's short day is closing fast,
    And sweet will be the rest of Heaven!

SEMPSTRESS'S HYMN

Day after day my weary task I ply,
  And half the night to ceaseless toil is given;
When weary is my heart and dim mine eye,
  I seem to hear the Saviour's voice from Heaven:
"Come unto Me, all ye by toil opprest,
  Come unto Me, and I will give you rest."

When all my labour scarce can bread procure,
  And weak with want my feeble fingers move;
When dear ones round me hunger's pangs endure,
  My drooping spirit hears that voice of love:
"Come unto Me, all ye by grief opprest,
  Come unto Me, and I will give you rest."

O Lord, how shall I come? my sinful heart
  Is prone to murmur, and Thy truth forget;
Dare I approach Thee, holy as Thou art?
  Methinks I hear that gentle whisper yet:
"Come unto Me, all ye by sin opprest,
  Come unto Me, and I will give you rest."

Oh, let me patiently await the day
  When Christ my Lord in glory shall appear,
When tears shall be for ever wiped away,
  And those who trust Him now His voice shall hear:
"Come, faithful servants, of My Father blessed,
  And I will give you everlasting rest."

RAGGED BOY'S HYMN

I would not take what is not mine, for hoards of wealth untold,—
Far better grasp the red-hot steel, than touch another's gold;
The love of money, God hath said, of evil is the root,
And if dishonesty thence spring, destruction is the fruit.

I would not take what is not mine, though none were near to see,
Conscience would my accuser stand, and God my judge would be;
The covetous desire, the wicked thought I would control,—
What shall it profit man to gain the world, and lose his soul?

I would not take another's goods,—the loser might repine,
His loss might heavy seem to him, but small compared to *mine;*
For oh! more precious far than all the wealth to nobles given,
An honest name, a quiet conscience, and the hope of Heaven!

I would not take what is not mine, but treasure seek above,
Gained without money, without price, from our Redeemer's love;
Time cannot change it, moth corrupt, nor thieves break through
    and steal,
And all eternity will but its boundless worth reveal!

RAGGED GIRL'S HYMN

The Sabbath sun has risen high,
    And sweetly sounds the Sabbath bell,
My basket now untouched must lie,
    This day I neither buy nor sell.
The Sabbath rest I will not break,
But God's commands my study make,
      And trust the word
      Of my dear Lord,
"I will not leave thee, nor forsake."

But I am poor, with none to aid,
    And Satan sore is tempting me,
"If thou give up the Sabbath trade,
    The Sabbath meal is not for thee."
My God, oh, let me never break
The least command that Thou didst make,
      But trust the word
      Of my dear Lord,
"I will not leave thee, nor forsake."

When Christ was faint with hunger's pain,
    The Tempter urged God's blessed Son
In way unmeet relief to gain;
    But steadfast stood the Holy One,
His perfect faith no doubt could shake,
The least command He would not break,
      He knew the love
      Of God above,
Would never leave Him, nor forsake.

Now, high in heaven, He hears and grants
    The prayers of those in faith who pray;
My earthly cares, my earthly wants,
    O Saviour, at Thy feet I lay:
Supply Thy servant's need, and make
Her soul of heavenly food partake,

For still, O Lord,
I trust Thy word,
"I'll never leave thee, nor forsake."

POLICEMAN'S HYMN

In the silence of night when the stars glimmer o'er me,
  The sound of my tread breaks the stillness alone,
I think of the far-distant mansions of glory,
  Where angels keep watch round the Holy One's throne.

Then, when clock after clock tells the hours that are fleeting,
  I think how each brings the day near and more near,
When around the dread judgment-seat multitudes meeting,
  The last solemn verdict of justice shall hear.

On the right hand will stand Christ's redeemed ones, possessing
  Robes washed in His blood, with His righteousness crowned;
On the left the lost souls that rejected the blessing;
  O God, in which number shall *I* then be found?

Am I resting my hopes on His infinite merit,
  Who suffered our pardon and peace to procure;
Am I seeking the aid of His life-giving Spirit
  To make my heart penitent, humble, and pure?

Oh! for those who believe there is "no condemnation,"
  The Judge shall Himself be their Saviour and Friend,
His voice shall award them eternal salvation,
  And bliss, in His presence, which never shall end.

PAUPER'S HYMN

Far from the friends to me most dear,
  Within the crowded ward I lie,
Destined, perhaps, mid strangers here
  To suffer and to die.
Time may all other joys remove
Yet leaves he still Faith, Hope, and Love.

Faith to the cross my spirit leads,
  And tells of One now glorified,
Who at the Father's right hand pleads
  For those for whom He died.
What trials can too bitter prove
While yet there rest Faith, Hope, and Love?

Hope whispers of that happy place
  Where I my Saviour shall behold,
And sing the wonders of His grace
  To harp of shining gold.
What sorrows can our patience move
While still remain Faith, Hope, and Love?

Love draws my heart towards my kind,
  Makes me in each a brother (or sister) see,
To cheer the sad, to help the blind,
  Are joys still left to me.
Bless my companions, heavenly Dove,
Fill them with Faith, and Hope, and Love.

There is no pain or sorrow here,
  For those who will God's lesson learn,
But *Faith* may brighten, *Hope* may cheer,
  And *Love* to blessing turn;
Then Peace descending from above
Unites with Faith, and Hope, and Love.

POSTMAN'S HYMN

In daily rounds my constant course I keep,
 Expected oft, but never asked to stay,
Nor know I who may laugh, or who may weep
 When gazing at the tidings I convey.
So is there one who comes to rich and poor,
 Expected long, unwelcome though he be;
When death's loud knock is sounding at my door,
 What are the tidings he will bring to me?

The haughty man to great possessions heir,
 The selfish man, whose treasure is below,
The selfish man all full of worldly care—
 To them his message is of fear and woe.
Bold Sabbath-breakers, scoffers at God's word,
 Who rush on paths which conscience must condemn,
When death's loud knock is at their dwellings heard,
 Oh! fearful tidings must he bring to them.

The contrite, mourning o'er repented sin,
 The meek in heart, whose treasure is above,
The faithful, who a heavenly crown would win—
 To such his message is of peace and love.
He comes to tell them that their griefs are o'er,
 That Christ from sin and sorrow sets them free;
Oh! when death's knock is sounding at my door,
 Such blessed tidings may he bring to me!

SERVANT'S HYMN

To whom do I obedience owe,
    Who should my willing service claim?
One master dwelling here below,
    And One above the starry frame.
Oh! may the thought of Him above,
    Each Christian servant's zeal awake,
To serve with faithfulness and love—
    For Christ, our heavenly Master's sake.

The earnest follower of the Lord,
    Must by the badge of truth be known,
Integrity that shrinks from fraud,
    And needs no eye—save God's alone
The cheerful heart, the ready mind
    That can in labour pleasure take,
To every kindly act inclined,
    For Christ, our heavenly Master's sake.

Though our best service is, we own,
    To God "unprofitable" still,
The Lord, to whom the heart is known,
    Rewards the attempt to do His will.
Oh! through His mercy may we rise,
    When the last trump our sleep shall break,
And find a welcome in the skies,
    For Christ, our heavenly Master's sake!

MINER'S HYMN

When verdant fields are seen no more,
    Where Heaven's beams can never shine,
Earth's hidden treasures to explore
    We labour in the gloomy mine.
But bright the torches' yellow rays
    That light us on our darksome way,
And sweet the voice of Hope that says,
    "We soon shall see the light of day."

And thus awhile must all mankind
    Toil on and labour here below,
Poor sinful mortals, weak and blind,
    And subject all to pain and woe.
But brightly shines God's holy Word
    Which lights us on our darksome way,
And sweet the hope its leaves afford,
    "We soon shall see a heavenly day."

The Lord of Angels deigned to come
    To bear our punishment and pain,
He made our dark abode His home,
    That we might rise, that we might reign.
And those who in His Word delight,
    Who trust His love, His will obey,
Shall shine in robes of spotless white
    In Heaven's everlasting day!

GARDENER'S HYMN

Ere our first parents fell, the ground
All beauty and abundance crowned;
But now the soil our labour needs,—
The *earth* produces thorns and weeds.

And trials on our pathway grow,
The prickly care, the stinging woe,
How oft the wounded spirit bleeds,—
Our *life* produces thorns and weeds.

But—worse than all—we find within,
The poisoned roots of pride and sin,
From them our misery proceeds,—
The *heart* produces thorns and weeds.

But, Lord, Thou bidst Thy sunbeams glow,
Thy gentle raindrops fall below;
When industry has dressed the bowers,
The *earth* produces fruits and flowers.

So when Thy love its radiance lends,
Thy Spirit like the dew descends,
When Faith, and Hope, and Peace are ours,
Our *life* produces fruits and flowers.

Oh! lead us to that blissful shore,
Where thorns and weeds are known no more,
Where Death can never reach the bowers,
To blast the fruit or blight the flowers!

LABOURER'S HYMN

I bless Thee, Lord, in early spring,
    When first the daisy decks the mead,
And in the furrowed ground we fling,
    With hope and prayer, the golden seed.
Let children in life's spring-time days
Lift up their hearts in prayer and praise!

I bless Thee in the summer heat,
    When cattle seek the cooling streams,
And o'er green fields of waving wheat
    The sun pours down his ripening beams.
Let man in life's bright summer days
Lift up his heart in prayer and praise!

I bless Thee in the autumn morn,
    When varied tints are on the leaves,
When gaily sounds the hunter's horn,
    Where reapers bind the golden sheaves.
Let man in life's declining days
Lift up his heart in prayer and praise!

I'll bless my God in winter's gloom,
    When Nature sleeps beneath the snow;
Oh! grant that when, beneath the tomb,
    My body lies in slumber low,
Thou wilt my soul to Heaven raise,
Where all is joy and all is praise!

WIFE'S HYMN

Help me, Lord Jesus, to fulfil
    The duties of a wedded wife,
Obedient to my husband's will,
    The joy and sunshine of his life.

Upon my brow no angry cloud,
    Upon my lips no hasty word,
Not one rebellious thought allowed,
    His wishes to my own preferred.

Help me to make my husband's home
    The calm abode of peace and love,
Where strife and discord ne'er may come,
    A type of that we seek above.

To walk together in Thy sight,
    To share each other's joys and woes,
Together pray at dawn of light,
    Together praise at evening's close;

Each ready, when temptation lowers,
    With gentle counsel, kindly aid;
Lord Jesus! let such lot be ours,
    Oh, bless the tie which Thou hast made!

United "until death us part,"
    Not death the Christian bond can sever;
Who love Thee here with faithful heart,
    With Thee shall live, and love for ever!

HYMN OF INDUSTRY

Not alone in God's house, or in seasons of prayer,
   Must the power of a Christian's religion be shown,
At his home, at his counter, and everywhere
   Must the strength of his faith by his actions be known;
For the clear path of duty is marked in God's Word,
"Be not slothful in business, but serving the Lord."

Not slothful in business! God wills that we toil,
   From the claims of our calling permits no retreat,
Though indolence may from the sentence recoil,
   "If the hand will not labour, the mouth should not eat;"
Faith to industry must but new motive afford,
"Be not slothful in business, but serving the Lord."

Yes, *serving the Lord;* 'mid our toils and our cares
   May we never forget the great Master we serve,
Who the mansions of light for His people prepares;
   For though man from his Maker can nothing *deserve,*
God hath graciously promised Himself to reward
Their labours of love who are "serving the Lord."

To the hand ever prompt in the business of life,
   But which never would close over fraudulent gain,
To the heart firm and strong in the world's busy strife,
   Which can holy, and humble, and faithful remain,
God in life and in death will His blessing accord,
"Be not slothful in business, but serving the Lord."

SOCIAL HYMN

How beautiful is Nature's face!
　　God made all things so fair,
Each keeps its own allotted place,
　　Nor hate, nor strife are there.
　　　　The hill and the plain,
　　　　　　The grass and forest tree,
　　　　The mighty waters of the main,
　　　　　　The lily on the lea,—
The sunny sky is over all,
　　And all is harmony.

So in the social world we stand
　　In God's appointed way,
And some He destines to command,
　　And others to obey.
　　　　The rich and the poor,
　　　　　　The lowly and the great,
　　　　The peasant at his cottage door,
　　　　　　The Sovereign in her state,—
One holy tie uniteth all
　　Who on one Master wait.

How glorious is the mountain height,
　　Whence kindly streamlets flow
To bless the peaceful valleys, bright
　　With bending corn below
　　　　The fair mountain-crown
　　　　　　Shall envy assail,
　　　　Or pride trample down
　　　　　　The harvest of the vale?—
The unity in Nature's world
　　In Man's world should prevail.

Oh! let not Satan overthrow
　　The order God designed;
The seeds of bitter envy sow.
　　And pride, among mankind.

Let rich love the poor,
   The humble bless the great,
The servant guard the master's store,
   The monarch serve the state,—
Each—in his separate sphere—to God
   His talents consecrate.

NATIONAL HYMN

O God of Hosts, our fathers' God,
  Thy blessing on our country shed,
Watch o'er the land our sires have trod,
  Watch o'er the land our sons will tread.

We pray for our Jerusalem,
  Keep discord from her homes afar,
Let thy strong arm deliver them
  From famine, pestilence, and war.

Though Britain spurns th' invader's sword
  As her white cliffs repulse the tide,
We would our grateful hearts, O Lord!
  Lift up in praise, and not in pride.

The race is not unto the swift,
  Nor is the battle to the strong;
Success and safety are Thy gift,
  The glory must to Thee belong.

Let our dear land in safety rest,
  Her people happy, loyal, free,
Blest amongst nations—still most blest
  In that pure faith which leads to Thee!

SOLDIER'S HYMN

A holy warfare, Lord, is mine
    Against a foe I cannot see,—
Oh! aid me with Thy grace divine,
    Thy faithful soldier let me be.

Thy armour—faith and righteousness,
    Thy holy Word within my hand,
When fierce temptations round me press
    Let me thy faithful soldier stand.

Should false shame lure me to deny
    The truth, or waver in the right,
Let me the insidious foe defy,
    And as Thy faithful soldier fight.

And oh! when death's keen shafts descend,
    And failing pulse, and glazing eye,
Warn that the conflict soon must end,
    Thy faithful soldier let me die!

Washed in Thy blood, let me appear
    Where crowns are to the conquerors given,—
Through Christ alone we triumph here,
    Or wear the victor's wreath in Heaven!

THE WISE MEN FROM THE EAST

"Where is thy new-born Lord, O Judah? Zion—where thy King?
The treasures of our distant land to Him we tribute bring;
Lo! in the East we saw His star, the day-spring from on high,
And we have come to worship Him enthroned in majesty!"

Thus spake the Eastern sages, thus the pious Gentiles spake,
But Judah would not know her Lord, His people would not wake;
The earth's Creator was on earth, unnoticed or forgot,
The Saviour came unto His own, His own received Him not.

The Gentile world that lay in darkness, they have seen the light,
Wherefore doth Zion turn away on whom it rose so bright!
Oh! thou that bearest joyful tidings, why so mute art thou?
Lift up thy voice, Jerusalem, behold thy Saviour now!

Oh! joy to those who seek Messiah while He may be found;
Again the heavenly harbinger sheds its soft lustre round,
Not on proud tower or stately palace streams the radiance mild,
But where the carpenter's meek wife bends o'er her blessed Child.

Hail, Mary, highly-favoured, hail! God's power o'ershadoweth thee,
Blessed amongst all women thou in thy humility!
Yea, rather blessed they who seek Christ's precepts to fulfil,—
His mother, brethren, sisters, they who know and do His will.

The sages to the infant Saviour bring their offerings meet,
Rich odours fill the perfumed air, gold glitters at His feet;
Oh! happy thus His poverty's sharp trial to defer,
To minister to Him who came to all to minister!

May we not deem when He in glory comes, th' eternal Lord
Will all those offerings of faith remember and reward,—
That richer than the wealth of worlds that hallowed gold will be,
Those sacred odours fragrance breathe through all eternity?

But now the Saviour sits enthroned above the Seraphim;
When all creation owns his sway, and angels worship Him,
Can *our* poor gifts acceptance find before His glorious throne?
The earth is His and all therein, not e'en our lives our own.

Lo! here the "Man of sorrows" representatives hath left,
The sick, the prisoners, the poor, of all but hope bereft;
Aid to "the least of these His brethren" to the Lord is given,
Off'rings of love to those He loves, He will accept in Heaven.

But still the noblest gift that man can lay before God's throne
Is the rich tribute of a heart that trusts in Him alone;
The poorest—least—this gift may bring, but oh! it will outweigh
The treasures of the universe upon the judgment day!

SONG OF HOPE

How highly blest were those who saw
    On earth their gracious Lord,
Who dared approach His sacred form,
    Who listened to His word,
Whose faith the Son of God approved,—
Whom the Redeemer saw, and loved!

Disciples hearkening to the voice
    Which reached the inmost soul,
That voice which could awake the dead,
    The winds and waves control;
Who heard—oh! more than happiness—
Those accents pardon, praise, or bless!

Who gazed on that soul-searching eye,
    Which every thought foresaw,
From whose calm power the hypocrite
    Shrank with instinctive awe,—
Yet saw on *them* its glances fixed
With tender mercy—love unmixed!

And may not such ecstatic bliss
    Be granted e'en to me?
Though death destroy this mortal flesh,
    These eyes my God shall see,
When coming in the clouds of light
His glory bursts upon my sight!

To hear the Saviour's voice of love
    Pronounce the gracious word,
"Come, blessed of My Father, come,
    Enter the kingdom of your Lord;"
To meet the smile in eyes divine—
Oh! can such rapture e'er be mine!

It may, it may, it is prepared
    For all who love Him here,
Who humbly search His written word,

And serve with faith and fear;
They all shall see Messiah's face
Radiant with glory, love, and grace!

The hand that guides their course on earth
    Shall wipe all tears away,
The light which cheers their thorny path
    Shall flash to perfect day;
Where Jesus reigns His saints shall be,
With Him through all eternity!

THE FEARFUL HEART

"Lord, careth Thou not that we perish!"
Cried his followers in agonized fear,
        When the black stormy sky,
        And the waves dashing high,
Made death with its terrors seem near.

The Saviour awoke from His slumber—
He spake, and rebuked the rude main;
        Though the wild cry for aid
        Feeble faith had betrayed,
E'en that cry was not uttered in vain.

"Lord, careth Thou not that we perish!"
This oft is the cry of despair,
        When affliction's waves roll,
        And the agonized soul
Scarce can breathe forth her anguish in prayer.

Yet the Saviour is watching beside us,
His eye cannot slumber or sleep,
        The bark which he guides
        Where His Presence abides
Can never be wrecked on the deep.

Oh! how soon would our inward griefs vanish,
Our souls fear no perils without,
        Could we hear His mild love
        Thus our terrors reprove,
"Ye of little faith, why did ye doubt?"

CONVICTION OF SIN

When Peter by the miracle
    Knew his celestial guest,
At the Redeemer's feet he fell
    By sense of guilt opprest;
"Depart!" he cried, subdued and awed,
"I am a sinful man, O Lord!"

So must the wisest, holiest, best,
    Their past transgressions own,
And on the Saviour's mercy rest
    Their hopes of heaven alone;
To all applies the suppliant word,
"Have mercy on a sinner, Lord!"

Can vain thoughts, covetous desires,
    And proud presumptuous hearts,
Endure the pure eye that requires
    Truth in the inward parts?
Self-righteousness, deluding sin,
Would shrink if light but streamed within.

Nor deem we good deeds can atone
    For one—the smallest—sin;
That virtues, in the balance thrown,
    May God's acceptance win,—
On tainted works man dare not rest,
"Unprofitable" at the best.

Ne'er be the impious hope allowed;
    No more let mortals aim
From God, or from themselves, to shroud
    Their helplessness and shame,
But at Thy feet, Lord Jesus, fall,
Like Peter, and confess it all!

The spotted leprosy of guilt
    Within we must have seen,
Ere we in faith cry, "If Thou wilt,

Lord! Thou canst make me clean!"
Oh! let us first our frailty see
Then find our cure, our all in Thee!

THE SACRED GUEST

When from the branches' leafy screen
    Zaccheus on his Master gazed,
What must his glad surprise have been
    When the Lord's eye to him was raised!
Christ singled out that one frail man
    From all the throng that round Him pressed,
And to the slighted publican
    These gracious words the Lord addressed.

"Make haste, descend, this day will I
    With thee abide." Zaccheus heard,
Received his Master joyfully,
    And reaped the blessing of that word:
"This day salvation to this home
    Is come," thus Christ the blessing gave;
"For lo! the Son of man is come
    That which was lost to seek and save!"

Mortal, on earth though low-esteemed,
    Thou, like the publican, mayst be;
The eye that on Zaccheus beamed
    May now be, *is* now fixed on thee.
From Him retirement is no screen,
    Thy insignificance no shroud;
And still all cold as thou hast been
    To thee the Saviour speaks aloud.

"Lo! at the door I stand and knock,
    If any open unto Me,
The portals of his heart unlock,
    I, even I, his Guest will be."
Oh! can that sacred Guest in vain
    Crave entrance to a sinner's heart;
Can pride itself unmoved remain,
    Or madness pray Him to depart?

No; sure with grateful joy alone
    Thou wilt thy Lord and Saviour meet,
Within thy heart prepare His throne,
    And pour thy treasures at His feet!
For think not Christ thy Guest can be
    Unless thy works His presence prove,
As in Zaccheus, God in thee
    See acts of justice, deeds of love.

Pure is the heart if God be there,
    That shrine no second lord receives;
Christ suffers not His "house of prayer"
    To be the shameful "den of thieves."
Far from the temple that He loves
    He drives base passions, selfish care,
With His own blood each stain removes,
    Then comes and dwells for ever there!

THE MOURNER

Forth from the city gate of Nain
   Slow wends the funeral array,
And friends by love or pity led
   Swell the procession on its way.
There from one closely shrouded form
   The deep low sobs convulsive burst—
The widow mourns her only son,
   And grief for her has done its worst.

The Saviour meets the sorrowing one,
   And they that bear the bier stand still,
The voice of grief is hushed in awe,
   And all in silence wait His will.
The "Man of Sorrows" sees her woe,
   He who knew grief, for grief can feel;
Weep not, thou mourner, Christ is near,
   As Man to pity, God to heal.

He speaks the word, and death obeys:
   Is it the breeze that stirs the shroud?
The stiffened limbs relax, they move
   With new and wondrous life endowed.
Life dawns upon the ashen cheek,
   Through each cold vein life's currents run,
The dead man rises from his bier—
   The widow clasps her living son!

Oh! ye bereaved ones, whose sad tears
   Some loved and lifeless form bedew,
The Eye that saw and pitied her
   Looks in compassion down on you;
Although no miracle at once
   Your loved one to your arms restore,
That voice which waked the widow's son
   Shall bid him live, to die no more.

THE CHRISTIAN BOND

When in our breasts we feel the flame of love,
    Kindled by heaven, becoming dim and low,
When cold our feelings are to God above,
    Unsympathizing to His poor below,
    When kindness seems a task, and words impatient flow;
How shall we cherish love's declining light?
    By drawing forth from memory's treasure-cave
The recollection of that mournful night
    When Jesus to the flock He died to save
    Gave His last mild commands, His parting blessing gave.

Muse on the solemn scene, till faith have power
    The inspired narrative to realize;
And round the board at evening's silent hour
    The chosen twelve appear, their anxious eyes
    Fixed on the Lamb of God, the spotless Sacrifice.
Lo! on the bread His sacred hand he lays,
    That hand so soon transfixed for them to be;
See the Redeemer's sad uplifted gaze,
    And hear the accents breathing mournfully,
    "This do ye in remembrance still of Me!"

Nor this the sole command by Christ then given
    To His disciples, loved unto the last,
At that sad meeting, when the Lord of Heaven
    Beheld death's awful hour approaching fast,
    The cross—the anguish which all mortal woe surpassed;
When He surveyed His small devoted band,
    And all that He for them would suffer knew,
The Saviour breathed that heavenly command,
    That bond of union to His faithful few,
    "Love one another e'en as I have loved you."

As I have loved you. Oh! more than love,—
    Language can breathe, and thought conceive no more;
It is not "as thyself"—*this* mounts above

All human feeling, bids us higher soar,
    Gaze on the cross, and feel the love a Saviour bore!
And can we ever rudely tear aside
    The band Messiah twined around His own?
Envy, resentment, petulance, or pride,
    Erase the mark by which His flock are known?
    Hath Christ ne'er loved *us*, to us no mercy shown?

THE CURE AT GETHSEMANE

The awful night hath passed, the day
  Soon o'er the mountains will be breaking,
And from their sleep of sorrow now
  The Saviour's followers are waking;
The Lord hath risen from His knees,
  His soul resigned on God relies,
The cup of vengeance now is full,
  The Victim waits the sacrifice.

Hark! hark! what sounds the stillness break,
  The clouds of danger darken o'er Him,
The traitor bands surround their Lord,
  And His betrayer stands before Him.
Then love bursts through the bonds of fear—
  Forth from the scabbard leaps the sword,
The apostle strikes the hasty blow
  To save—or to avenge his Lord!

Oh! many a miracle of love
  The Lord had wrought for souls believing,
Now stilling storms, now by His power
  The wants of multitudes relieving;
But the last miracle of Christ,
  Ere to His fearful trial brought,
Was wrought when captive and betrayed—
  And for His persecutor wrought.

He touched the wound—and it was healed;
  Oh! deed, unmeasured love revealing;
Ere it was nailed upon the cross
  That gracious hand's last touch was healing!
And when the lighter wrongs we bear
  Rouse in our hearts vindictive fire,
Shall not remembrance of that deed
  Thrill on our souls, and calm our ire?

Sweet are the thoughts that wondrous cure
    Wrought at Gethsemane may yield us;
We, too, were rebels to our King,
    And He, though rebels, touched and healed us.
Let us to all men mercy show,
    As we through only mercy live;
Rejoice, like Christ, the poor to bless,
    Like Christ, the guilty to forgive!

HYMN FOR THE COMMUNION

At the foot of the Cross where my Saviour is bleeding,
  By faith let me now with His followers bend;
Let me hear for my pardon His voice interceding,
  And see, for my sins, these dear life-drops descend.

As when His fierce murderers mocked and defied Him,
  The Maries still clung to their Master adored,
Nor for thrones would have quitted their station beside Him,
  Their long mournful watch by their crucified Lord;

So, unmoved by the scoffs of the foe and blasphemer,
  I would muse upon all that my Saviour hath borne;
Permitted to watch by the dying Redeemer,
  And gaze on that pale brow encircled with thorn.

Oh! let such remembrance be present before me
  When called on the feast of His love to partake,
Let my spirit commune with her Lord now in glory,
  And trembling behold what He bore for our sake!

HYMN FOR THE DYING

The day of life is closing,
    Its last faint beam has fled;
Yet faith, on Christ reposing,
    Can Death's cold waters tread;
The dark sea spreads before me,
    Upon the brink I stand;
Oh, guide me, Lord of Glory,
    To Heaven's blissful strand!
      To Thee, Lord, I flee,
      My trust is in Thee;
"O death, where is thy sting? O grave, thy victory?"

No longer here detain me,
    I hear my Saviour's voice,
I feel His arm sustain me,
    I triumph and rejoice!
The Lord will bless for ever
    Those who His love have known,
Nor life, nor death shall sever
    The Saviour from His own!
      Victorious and free
      His people shall be;
"O death, where is thy sting? O grave, thy victory?"

DEATH IS NOT DREADFUL

Death is not dreadful, no!
   Though sad affection weeps,
The grave is but the cradle where
   The future seraph sleeps,
And smiling Faith her watch above
   The peaceful slumberer keeps.

Death is not dreadful, no!
   'Twere terrible to die,
E'en to the best, if called to stand
   Before the Deity
Bare in their guilt,—without a friend
   To meet the Judge's eye.

But oh! the weakest saint
   May fearless pass the flood,
His robe shall shine as white as light
   Washed in his Saviour's blood;
The Judge Himself shall plead his cause,
   Who as his Surety stood.

Death is not dreadful, no!
   It bids us reap at last
The joyful harvest of our tears,
   Our toils and trials past;
It gives us our inheritance,
   How glorious and how vast!

Death is not dreadful, no!
   It is the Saviour's voice
Calling His lambs unto the fold;
   They hear it, and rejoice:
In life or death "to be with Christ"
   This is His servants' choice.

So, when the long night comes,
   In peace they close their eyes,
Humbly confiding in His care

Whose love all change defies,—
Bowing to His Almighty will,
   All-merciful, All-wise.

Then welcome be the night
   Preceding endless day,
Thrice blessed the Gospel's glorious light,
   That chased its gloom away,
And showed us life beyond the tomb
   In Christ, the sinner's Stay.

NEVER FORSAKEN

Why dread the future, trembling one,
    Since whatsoe'er the griefs it bring,
A Father's voice pronounced the fate
    It bears upon its rapid wing?
Canst thou not trust thy earthly hopes
    To Him in whom thy soul confides;
Nor cast thy cares upon thy Lord
    When angels whisper "God provides."

"Why for the morrow take ye thought?"
    The God of truth and mercy said;
His gracious arm supports thee now,
    His sheltering wing is o'er thee spread;
He ne'er forgets His human pangs—
    The stricken soul, the tortured limb—
Nor gives a moment's needless pain
    To those who love and trust in Him!

What dost thou fear, what dost thou dread?
    The rushing wind—the billow's roar?
The gale, though rude, by love is sent
    To speed thy course to Heaven's shore.
More fatal were a death-like calm;
    The stormy voyage not long can last,
The Saviour's welcome overpays
    A thousand-fold the perils past.

Fear not,—what should God's children fear?
    The dreaded clouds may roll away;
Unnumbered mercies oft received
    Should strengthen faith to trust today.
Enough—without the Lord's consent
    None from thy head one hair can sever;
Enough—thou art the Almighty's care;
    Afflicted, but forsaken never!

THY FATHER'S FRIEND

Forsake not thou thy father's friend,
    Forsake not thou thine own;
Though care and grief his form may bow,
And frosts of age be on his brow,
And like a leafless willow now
    He stand on earth alone.

Forsake not thou thy father's friend,
    Revere the hoary head;
Thou may'st have little to bestow
To lessen want, or lighten woe,
But who does not the solace know
    Which kindly words can shed!

Forsake not thou thy father's friend;
    So when thy strength is o'er,
May'st thou ne'er want a friend in need,
Thy age to cheer, thy footsteps lead,
But he who is a "Friend indeed"
    Be thine for evermore!

FEAR OF GOD AND FEAR OF MAN

The fear of God most high—
    It is a holy fear;
It makes us pass through life as those
    Who know their Lord is near.
The fear of sinful man—
    'Tis a debasing fear,
Shame will be theirs who dare not brave
    A censure or a sneer.

It was the fear of God
    By which the Hebrews three
Undaunted met the tyrant's frown—
    Unmoved the flames could see.
It was the fear of man
    Weak Pilate's breast within,
That stained his hands with guiltless blood,
    His soul with blackest sin.

No courage is like that
    Which steadfast faith bestows;
With God our Friend, we would be safe
    Were all the world our foes!
Faith but the *duty* sees
    Where doubt would danger scan;
'Tis through the fear of God alone
    We crush the fear of man.

THE SINNERS' PORTION

Who Wisdom's path forsakes
    Leaves all true joy behind;
He who the peace of others breaks,
    No peace himself shall find.
Flowers above and thorns below,
Little pleasure, lasting woe,
Such is the fate that sinners know.

The drunkard gaily sings
    Above his foaming glass,
But shame and pain the revel brings
    Ere many hours can pass.
Flowers above and thorns below,
Little pleasure, lasting woe,
Such is the fate that sinners know.

The thief may count his gains;—
    If he the sum could see
Of future punishment and pains,
    Sad would his reckoning be.
Flowers above and thorns below,
Little pleasure, lasting woe,
Such is the fate that sinners know.

The Sabbath-breaker spurns
    What Wisdom did ordain;
God's rest to Satan's use he turns,
    A blessing to a bane.
Flowers above and thorns below,
Little pleasure, lasting woe,
Such is the fate that sinners know.

O Lord, to Thee we pray,
    Do Thou our faith increase,
Make us to walk in Wisdom's way,

The only way of peace!
For flowers above and thorns below,
Little pleasure, lasting woe,
Such is the fate that sinners know.

DEATH-BED HYMN

Standing upon the awful brink,
Almost too faint to pray or think,
Thou who canst pain and fear control,
My God, have mercy on my soul!

A chilling gloom I feel within,
A trembling consciousness of sin;
I cannot to my mind recall
What sins—but Thou hast marked them all.

Oh, let my soul some promise hear
From Thy blest Word to calm her fear;
Oh, bid this doubt, this anguish cease—
My Saviour say, "Depart in peace!"

Thou know'st I loved Thee,—weak might be
My faith—but it was fixed on Thee;
Thou didst a gracious promise make—
Oh, save me for Thy mercy's sake!

Methinks I hear my Lord reply:
"Fear not, for I am ever nigh;
In life—in death—beyond the grave—
My arm shall guide, support, and save.

"Thy ransom hath been paid by love,
Thy mansion is prepared above;
No power of death, or hell, or sin,
From Me one pardoned soul shall win!"

SAVE ONE!

Souls are perishing before thee,
  Save—save one!
It may be thy crown of glory,
  Save—save one!
From the waves that would devour,
From the raging lion's power,
From destruction's fiery shower,
  Save—save one!

Not in thine own strength confiding,
  Save—save one;
Faith and prayer thy efforts guiding,
  Save—save one!
None can e'er, unless possessing
Heavenly aid and heavenly blessing,
To the work of mercy pressing,
  Save e'en one.

Who the worth of souls can measure?
  Save—save one!
Who can count the priceless treasure?
  Save—save one!
Like the stars shall shine for ever
They who faithfully endeavour
Dying sinners to deliver,
  Save—save one!

NEW YEAR'S HYMN

WRITTEN AT THE TIME OF THE INDIAN MUTINY, 1857.

In the year that hath passed o'er us,
    Many suffered woe and pain;
Time can ne'er the brave restore us,
    Far in distant India slain.
        Praying, praising,
    Saints have joined the martyr-train.

But another year is dawning,
    We are spared its light to see;
May each blessing, may each warning,
    Draw us nearer, Lord, to Thee—
        Like Thy martyrs
    Faithful unto death to be!

May Thy Word, salvation bringing,
    Shine where darkness now appears;
Plenteous be the harvest springing,
    That was sown in blood and tears;—
        Light from darkness,
    Joy from sorrow, hope from fears!

Blessed hope now set before us,
    Satan's slaves shall burst their thrall,
All the nations join the chorus
    To the Lord who died for all;—
        Ransomed millions
    At the Saviour's feet shall fall!

POEMS.

THE INDIAN MAID

The leading incidents in this poem are historical. The descendants
of Pocahontas are still to be found, I believe, in the United States.

Through the majestic forest shade
    The light of morn is faintly shining,
Scarce struggling through the twilight made
    By leafy boughs entwining;
As Nature, from the birth of Time,
    Deep in this lone sequestered wood,
Had formed herself a bower sublime,
    Where she might dwell with solitude,
And list the wild bird's note, nor fear
Man's guilty foot could wander here,
Or war's unhallowed trumpet wake
The slumbering echoes, rudely break
The solemn, deep, unearthly still,
Which to a stranger's soul must thrill
A sense of awe—as though he trod
A temple consecrate to God!

Yet war can penetrate e'en here
    To blight the beauties of creation,
Till Nature's calmest scenes appear
    Dark haunts of desolation.
The murderer's sword hath left the sheath,
    When from the bright pure heaven above,
And smiling earth, there seemed to breathe
    But peace, and joy, and love.
And even now, when blushing morn,
On rosy clouds by zephyrs borne,
Comes in her laughing loveliness
The world to brighten and to bless,
It were more meet that heaven should shroud
Her radiant brow in some dark cloud,
And dewy tears of morning flow
For scenes of blood on earth below!

See, in the forest's thickest maze
    The dark-eyed Indian tribes assembling,
Free as the pure fresh breeze that plays
    On leaves around them trembling.
Wild Nature's wilder sons,—each brow
    The radiant sun of western lands
Hath kindled to a redder glow;
    In painted pride the savage stands,
So differing in garb—in skin—
In mien—he scarce might seem akin
To Europe's sons, did we not trace
In the dark features of his face
The same fierce passions, which declare
The race of Adam here and there,
And prove, alas! we share with all
One common origin, and fall!

But what white-bosomed victim here
    Stands bound, a cruel death awaiting,
The dreadful preparations near
    Now firmly contemplating,—
Now raising calm his thoughtful eye
    Where, through the boughs that intervene
Of Nature's verdant canopy,
    Bright glimpses are of heaven seen?
Reflects he on the murderous doom
Which destines him a bloody tomb,
Sudden cut off, before his time,
In honour's course, in manhood's prime,—
On projects that with him must die,
Hopes ripening to reality,
But blasted ere their fruits afford
To science its well-earned reward?

Or thinks he on the distant land
    To which life's earliest ties have bound him,

Where last he grasped his father's hand,
    And felt his mother's arms around him?
Above these savage yells of death
    Does memory hear the low deep prayer
Her trembling lips could scarcely breathe,
    That God might shield him everywhere?
'Tis answered, yes, that prayer of love,
Scarce heard on earth, has reached above!
Though fixed his doom, though Death e'en now
Stands prompt—he may not strike the blow!
Twice did the trembling compass[1] give
A respite,—wonder bade him live;
But other succour now must save
The hero from untimely grave.

For lo! behold, with savage joy
    His foes their victim now surrounding,
Eager to smite and to destroy,
    The woods with yells resounding!
Calm and resigned he kneels in dust,
    Lays on the stone his manly head,
And waits the crushing blows, that must
    Number him with the dead;
When, like the bright celestial bow
Which, when the angry tempests blow,
And heaven's bolts from high are hurled—
Speaks peace and mercy to the world—
Forward there springs an Indian maid,
As light as fawn in forest glade,
Her cheek with generous ardour glowing,
O'er her slight form the dark hair flowing,
While firm resolve, and feeling high,
Sparkle in her soul-speaking eye.

---

1 Captain Smith, the captive here mentioned, twice diverted the Indians from their murderous intentions, by drawing their attention to the marvels of the needle.

"O Father, spare the chief!" she cries,
    Before her parent interceding,
Her clasped hands, and eloquent eyes,
    More than her accents pleading;
"Was he not brave in war, and kind
    And true in peace? did he e'er break
The solemn wampum league, or bind
    The captive to the stake?
For him a wife afar may sigh,
A lonely mother mourning die,
For who shall now with sounding bow
Bring down for them the elk or roe,
Whose hatchet shall defend their home
When hostile tribes with war-cries come?
Oh! spare the white chief, that his voice
His wife's sad bosom may rejoice;
Oh! spare him, that his hand may dry
The teardrop in his mother's eye!"

But stern the Indian's answer; vain
    Her pleading words, her warm endeavour,
The murderers' clubs are raised again
    To crush the brave for ever!
Lo! from her knees the maiden springs,
    Rapid as lightning's flash above,
As guardian angels spread their wings
    O'er mortals that they love,
Around the Doomed her arms are thrown,
His form protected by her own,
With him will she the worst await,
And save his life, or share his fate!
"Strike him!" she cries, "but 'neath the blow
His blood and mine shall mingled flow;
Strike him! but in the spirit-land
With him shall Pocahontas stand,

Nor live to say her tribe hath slain
The chief for whom she prayed in vain!"

There is a spell in woman's eye
 When, injured Virtue's cause defending,
Her soul is roused to energy,
 Vigour with sweetness blending!
Soft plumes that tremble in the air
 Have formed a breastplate strong to save,
And woman's heart will oft-times dare
 What might appal the brave!
E'en the rude Indians feel the power
Of courage equal to the hour,
Catch virtues warm inspiring glow
And more than mercy asked, bestow.
Rise, Briton, rise, both safe and free,
With life receive back liberty;
Spring from the spot of sacrifice
From which thou ne'er didst hope to rise;
Or rather, once more prostrate fall
To bless the God who saved from all!

Not long the dark-eyed maiden hears
 His grateful words of deep devotion,
They part—to meet in future years
 Beyond the heaving ocean.
"Go, stranger, to thy distant home,"
 Thus flowed her simple, wild farewell,
"When thy pale tribes to greet thee come,
 Then of the Red man's mercy tell!
And when the round sun leaves the sky
To light the Indian forests high,
Say thou hast left a daughter there,
And bid him here thy greetings bear!
And oh! if e'er a Red man be
Thy captive, then remember me;

If weary-footed Indian pray
For shelter, turn not thou away,
But to my race a father be,
As thou hast found a child in me!"

Sweet maid! she little dreamed how near
    The hour when she—a captive mourning—
A Briton's voice her grief would cheer,
    The White man's debt returning;
When Rolfe with tenderest care essayed
    The maiden's flowing tears to dry,
Until captivity he made
    More sweet than liberty!
Amidst her grief, amidst her fear,
Love's melting tones first reached her ear,
And oh! has life one dark distress
That sweet voice cannot soothe or bless!
It was as though the raging blast
Had o'er some silent harp-strings past,
And waked so soft, so wild a strain
(As joy still owes its zest to pain),
The spirit of the storm drew near,
Closed his dark wings, and paused to hear!

And with Rolfe's heart she learned to share
    His hopes, on heavenward pinion soaring,
And with him knelt in humble prayer,
    The Christian's God adoring.
The sacred tie has made them one,
    That tie which death alone can part,
Love's circlet on her hand hath shone,
    Love's torch within her heart;
And she hath quitted that wild shore
Her tearful eyes shall view no more,
And, wafted by the western wind,
Left all that once she loved behind.

Honours in Albion's isle attend
The Indian bride, the captive's friend;
From royal lips[1] her praises sound,
Her generous deed with fame is crowned.
But precious to her soul, above
All fame, her husband's smile of love,
Or Smith's proud glance, when she would claim
Once more a daughter's cherished name.

But oh! how close the sacred ties
    That to our native country bind us,
In foreign scenes the heart still sighs
    For dearer left behind us!
She longed to see the waving woods,
    Her dark-haired sire, her Indian shore,
Her spirit yearned to cross the floods
    And view her native soil once more.
But ere the vessel left the strand,
Sickness, with damp and heavy hand
Stayed the fair wanderer, like a spell
Unseen, but irresistible,
For death in his pale bark had come
To waft her to a brighter home.
Brief was the passage, but how vast
The space in those short seconds past!
One moment Rolfe in wild distress
Hung o'er her fading loveliness,
Met her long dying gaze of love,
Saw her pale lips in blessing move,
The next—and her immortal soul
Had crossed the floods, and reached the goal,
And he was left to mourn its flight,
Till death, that severed them, should reunite!

---

1 Pocahontas was presented to James I.

BLANCHE

Life's deep afflictions not alone demand
    Devout submission to th' Almighty's will,
The flower nursed by dew, by breezes fanned,
    Yet may the slow-corroding canker kill,
    While all around it smiles, it fadeth still;
Such is the thankless heart which—pleasure-cloyed—
    Turns from surrounding good to fancied ill,
And forms within itself a cheerless void
'Mid blessings unacknowledged, pleasures unenjoyed.

Oh! deem ye not them sufferers alone
    Whom poverty consumes, or cares oppress,
Who mourn o'er health departed, hopes o'erthrown,
    Or—severed from a parent's fond caress—
    Find the world changed into a wilderness;
As deep the desolation of a mind
    (With all to cheer it, and with all to bless)
That, to its own self-fostered gloom resigned,
Rejects the happiness God bade it seek and find.

My parents, faithful soldiers of the Cross,
    Had o'er successive offspring closed the tomb,
And—ere my infant heart could know its loss—
    They too had sunk beneath the mortal doom,—
    My life, in sorrow passed, commenced in gloom.
Yet friends were left; the patriarch of our line
    For my sake would a parent's cares resume,
And his mild consort, then in life's decline,
As she had watched my father's youth would watch o'er mine.

With tenderness did they their charge fulfil,
    In the retirement of a peaceful spot;
But ah! not theirs the strength to curb the will,
    To train Christ's soldier for a trying lot.
    Offences gently chidden—and forgot,
The wavering denial, weak delay,
    And threat—by punishment succeeded not,

Marred in the morn the promise of the day,
The Christian child's first lesson should be to *obey*.

Cruel, misjudging tenderness! how soon
    The plant by weakness nursed bore fruit in woe!
The branch which love with gentle hand might prune,
    Reserved to fall 'neath God's chastising blow!
    Can they the toils of warfare undergo
Whose childhood knows no wish ungratified?
    Oh! check the first advances of the foe,
Stay at the source the quickly-swelling tide,—
From reason's dawn must thou for good or ill decide.

Time fleeted by,—I was a child no more,
    But with my growth, alas! the evil grew.
I loved creation's wonders to explore,
    But on the world within ne'er fixed my view.
    Eager the paths of science to pursue,
By praise encouraged, and by pride impelled,
    The charmed task each day would I renew,
And, while my bosom with vainglory swelled,
Measured myself by those I deemed that I excelled.

And was I happy? no, the unbridled mind
    May soar too freely through the fields of air,
In its own liberty a bondage find;
    My spirits were not bound by earthly care,
    No loss had I to weep, no frowns to bear.
My own enjoyment was my single aim,
    I sought it upon earth, nor found it there,
Satiety and disappointment came,—
"Oh, that I were a man to win the meed of fame!"

I longed for something lofty—undefined—
    A kindred soul to mingle with my own,
A destiny more worthy of a mind
    Now amidst uncongenial spirits thrown.
    By friends surrounded—yet I stood alone:

Self was the gilded idol I adored;
    Had I Christ's strength and my own weakness known,
Soon had that idol felt the gospel sword,
Low levelled in the dust before my conquering Lord!

Yet was I ardent in religious cause,
    Impiety I scorned—denounced—despised;
No warrior his holy weapon draws
    With zeal more fervent than I exercised
    When faithlessness in others I chastised;
My spirit kindled at the martyr's tale,
    There were my dreams of glory realized;
Oh! where their faith prevailed would mine prevail,
Could soul so ardent in the fiery trial fail?

I felt not then that in life's loneliest way
    A glorious warfare may the Christian wage;
Humbly to honour, meekly to obey,
    In charity's mild duties to engage,
    And gently soothe the fretfulness of age,—
Such is the sacred post to woman given;
    Home is her battle-field; the strife must rage
Till sin and self are from their empire driven:
Will not the victor rest with martyr-saints in heaven?

With weariness I viewed my rural life,
    Hid from a world in which I hoped to shine,—
Better the press of care, the toil of strife,
    Than thus in an insipid calm to pine,
    Watching my aged guardian's slow decline;
Youth was, I deemed, the season for delight,
    E'en should its sorrows with its joys be mine,
The deepest shadows mark the brightest light,
Dim is the hour when both in one dull hue unite!

Sin may invite the soul; by discontent
    The wayward soul herself inviteth sin;
I sought a trial—God the trial sent.

One formed a colder heart than mine to win,
    Lighted the soul-consuming torch within:
Montoro sought my hand, his lips revealed
    His love; I felt another life begin,—
To fervent love must self his empire yield,—
No, for that love itself was selfishness concealed!

What though Montoro's highborn parents frowned
    Upon his union with a lowly maid;
Though upon means already slender found,
    A second burden thus would now be laid,—
    Although with darkened sight, and strength decayed,
My widowed grandsire claimed a daughter's care,—
    What was it to a soul by passion swayed?
His lonely dwelling now must strangers share,
No daughter's voice to raise the hymn, or join the prayer.

'Twas on a summer morn I left my home,
    Buoyant with hope and long-sought happiness,
Yet did a feeling of misgiving come
    When, folded in the old man's last caress,
    He in his trembling accents strove to bless
The child who left him lonely, aged, and blind
    E'en then my bosom would the thought oppress,
"Deserter from the post by God assigned,
Wilt thou again on earth a love so faithful find?"

'Twas but a transitory thought; my soul
    Exulted in an earthly paradise;
Impetuous hope had reached its wished-for goal,
    And I could bear to see the tear-drops rise
    Within those dear and venerable eyes,
Could joyous from my childhood's home depart;
    For him I loved too great no sacrifice,
Care had no weight, and poverty no smart;
He was the treasure of my soul, the idol of my heart!

Time roused me slowly from my golden dream,

Love, born in smiles, survived to mourn in tears;
Earth's brightest blessings are not what they seem;
   Beneath the sober influence of years
   Fancy's gay blossoms fade, and truth appears.
When word or frown impatient care betrayed,
   My wounded soul could not disguise her fears
That now my lord with colder feelings weighed
And felt the sacrifice which blinded love had made.

And what I felt I spoke; my untamed soul
   The task of patient love had yet to learn,
Each word, each look, each feeling to control,
   Harshness with meek submission to return,
   By charms more lasting, love more lasting earn,
This to my spirit was a task unknown;
   My lip would quiver, and my cheek would burn,
By glance reproachful and upbraiding tone
I marred Montoro's happiness—and crushed my own.

Hardships and cares, by eager love defied,
   Heavy upon my weary spirit pressed,—
The struggle between poverty and pride,—
   Ill could my temper bear the bitter test,
   Exhausted hope could find no place of rest;
I, for the love of one, had all resigned,
   And now my heart in bitterness confessed,
Though faithful love might yet remain behind,
It was no more the light of joy, the sunbeam of the mind.

Yet I content, nay, happy might have proved,
   Could I have meekly stooped the yoke to bear,
Nor sought perfection in the man I loved;
   But I had hoped a heaven on earth to share,—
   Too ardent hope rebounds into despair.
When pride or passion fix the nuptial chain,
   Time must the gilding from the fetters wear,—
Love's golden links alone unchanged remain,
Hallowed by faith, to be renewed in Heaven again.

I now approach the crisis of my woes.
 One, known in early life, again I met;—
With proud disdain I had regarded those
  Who—low by birth, by nature lower—yet
  Their upstart confidence in riches set;
And could I calmly Agnes now behold
 Her brow encircled with a coronet,
Endure her haughty smile, her greeting cold,
Who owed her triumph solely to the power of gold?

I felt the press of poverty, and she
 Had only to desire—and to possess;
Yet why should sight of her prosperity
  Add to my cup one drop of bitterness?
  Her luxuries made not my comforts less.
I know it now, though my deluded heart
 Would then have scorned its weakness to confess;
Envy had fixed within his venomed dart,
And love had no sweet balm to heal the wounded part.

Hate's ready weapon, ridicule, I sought,
 The lightest word may give the deepest wound,—
Montoro's sparkling wit the impulse caught,
  His jests, by malice circulated round,
  Too soon a fatal destination found.
Words are but breath, but breath may kindle flame
 Destined to level cities with the ground!
My God, from Thy dread wrath the judgment came,
But oh! my guilt, my wretchedness were still the same!

A fatal sword hung o'er my head unknown,
 Yawned at my feet a precipice unseen!
One morn Montoro had gone forth alone,
  Methought there was a sadness in his mien,
  And tender had his words at parting been;
A long fond kiss upon our babe he prest,
 Still in her cradle slumbering serene;

The tide of love gushed warmer in my breast,
His glance recalled the hours when first that love was blest.

Thrice the accumulating mound of sand
   Marked in my glass the hours that passed away,
I turned it listlessly with weary hand,
   And marvelled at Montoro's long delay:
   Heavy with mist and rain advanced the day;
My babe awoke and wept, her cry of fear
   I strove to soothe with melancholy lay,
And bore her, sobbing, to the casement near,
And bade her infant accents call her father dear.

Upon the dreary prospect forth I gazed;
   Poured from the lowering sky incessant rain,
The trees their dark and dripping branches raised,
   Reflected dimly on the flooded plain,
   Trickled the raindrops down the misty pane;
The wind in sudden gusts our dwelling shook,
   Then sank, in mournful murmurs to complain;
With heavy heart the casement I forsook,
While to my early home her flight sad memory took.

"Where is the happiness I thought to find
   When forth I went, a young rejoicing bride?
Springs grief from earthly trials, or a mind
   For ever restless and dissatisfied?
   Montoro's love outweighed the world beside,—
Is it his wife's misfortune or her sin
   That petty cares so oft our hearts divide?
Oh, that another era might begin,
And life's storms but enhance the holy peace within!

"My childhood's friend I in his age forsook,—
   The old man sleeps beneath the grassy sod!
To frown of care is changed the joyous look
   With which Montoro once life's garden trod;
   God gave me life,—I have not lived to God!

My threefold duties I neglected see,—
    Great God! suspend awhile thy chastening rod!
Oh, come, my husband, life henceforth shall be
Devoted unto piety and thee!"

He came—but oh! *how* did Montoro come?
    Why did I live to look on his return?
Bleeding and pale they bore him to his home.
    Life glimmered faintly,—I had yet to learn
    The hopeless grief that must for ever burn
Within the widow's desolated breast:
    Enough—mine eyes have seen Montoro's urn;
One tie is left—one treasure still possest,—
The shadow of despair is cast on all the rest!

There is no wretchedness where sin is not,—
    Religion may relieve the darkest woes,
All—save remorse—be softened or forgot—
    But where can she—the guilty—find repose,
    Whose anguish from her own transgression flows?
My pride—*my* envy bade Montoro die,
    His life embittered, stained with blood its close!
Aye, weep ye who *can* weep—but I—but I
My heart weeps tears of blood, and yet mine eyes are dry!

PRIDE

Proud—and of what! poor vain and helpless worm
Crawling in weakness through thy life's brief term,
Yet filled with thoughts presumptuous, bold, and high,
As though thy grovelling soul could scan the sky,
As though thy wisdom, which can not foreshow
What *one* day brings of coming weal or woe,
Could pierce the depths of far futurity,
And all the winged shafts of fate defy!

Art proud of riches? of the glittering dust
Each day *may* rob thee of, and one day *must*,
When mines of wealth will purchase no delay,
When dust to dust must turn, and clay to clay,
And nought remain to thee of all possest,
Save one dark cell in earth's unconscious breast!
Or proud of power? on this little ball
Some petty tract may thee its master call,
Some fellow-mortals, bending lowly down,
Bask in thy smile, or tremble at thy frown;
Great in the world's eyes, in thine own how great,
How swells thy breast with conscious pride elate!

And art thou great? lift up—lift up thine eyes,
Survey the heavens, gaze into the skies,—
View the fair worlds that glitter o'er thy head,
Orb above orb in bright succession spread,
Beyond the reach of sight, the power of thought,—
Then turn thy gaze to earth, and thou art—*nought;*
The globe itself a speck—an atom thou!
Oh, child of dust, shall pride exalt thee now?
In one thing only thou mayst glory still,
And let exulting joy thy bosom fill,—
Glory in this—and what is all beside,—
That for this worm—this atom—Christ hath died!

Does conscious genius fire thy haughty mind,

Genius, that raises man above his kind,
The lofty soul that soars on wing of fire,
While crowds at distance marvel and admire?
Oh! while the charmed world pays her homage just,
Remember *every talent is a trust,*
A treasure God doth to thy care confide,
A cause for gratitude, but none for pride.
If thou that precious talent misapply,
To spread the flood of infidelity,
To strew with flowers the paths which sinners tread,
To hide one treacherous snare by Satan spread,—
How blest, how great, compared to thee, the man
Whose life obscurely ends as it began,
To whose meek soul no knowledge ere was given
Save that—of all most high—that lifts the soul to Heaven.
For, as the sun's pure radiance, streaming bright,
Transcends the glow-worm's dim and fading light,
The wisdom to that man vouchsafed from high
Excels the earth-born fires that flash—and die!

Oh! where shall pride securely harbour then,
Where urge his claims to rule the minds of men?
Blest Eden knew him not,—where all was fair,
Where all was faultless,—pride abode not there.
The glorious angels are above his sway,
Their bliss to minister—to serve—obey;
We—only we—poor children of a day,
Tread haughtily the ground for our sakes curst,
And wear with pride the chains our Surety burst!
Would that the world could know and truly prize
That which is great in the Creator's eyes!
The poor man, bending o'er his scanty store,
Who, with God's presence blest, desires no more;
Who feels his sins, his weakness, though his ways
Be just and pure beyond all *human* praise;

Whose humble thoughts well with his prayer accord,
"Have mercy upon me, a sinner, Lord!"
Who, heir of an eternal, heavenly throne,
Rests all his hopes on Christ, and Christ *alone!*
Wisest of men—for he alone is wise;
Richest of men—secure his treasure lies;
Greatest of men—his mansion is on high;
His Father—God; his portion—immortality!

A DREAM OF THE SECOND ADVENT

I dreamed that in the stilly hush of night—
Deep midnight—I was startled from my sleep
By a clear sound as of a trumpet! Loud
It swelled, and louder, thrilling every nerve,
Making the heart beat wildly, strangely, till
All other senses seemed in hearing lost.
Up from my couch I sprang in trembling haste,
Cast on my garments, wondering to behold
Through half-closed shutters sudden radiance gleam,
More clear, more vivid than the glare of day!
What marvel, then, that with a breathless hope
That gave me wings, forth from my home I rushed,
Though heaved the earth as if instinct with life,
Its very dust awakening! Can it be—
Is this the call, "Behold the Bridegroom comes!"
Comes He, the long-expected—long-desired?
Crowds thronged the street, with every face upturned,
Gazing into the sky—the flaming sky—
Where every cloud was like a throne of light.
None could look back, not even to behold
If those beloved were nigh; one thrilling thought
Rapt all the multitude—"Can HE be near!"

Then cries of terror rose—I scarcely heard;
And buildings shook, and rocked, and crashing fell—
I scarcely marked their fall; the trembling ground
Rose like the billowy sea—I scarcely felt
The motion, such intensity of hope—
Joy—expectation—flooded all my soul,
A tide of living light, o'erwhelming all
The hopes and fears, the cares and woes of earth!
Could any doubt remain? Lo! from afar
A sound of "Hallelujah!" ne'er before
Had mortal ear drunk in such heavenly strain,
Save when on Bethlehem's plain the shepherds heard

The music of the skies!
     Behold! behold!
Like white-winged angels rise the radiant throng
That from yon cemetery's gloomy verge
Have burst, immortal—glorious—undefiled!
Bright as the sun their crowns celestial shine,
Yet I behold them with undazzled eye!
Oh! that yon glittering canopy of light
Would burst asunder, that I might behold
Him whom so long, not seeing, I have loved!
It parted—lo! it opened—as I stood
With clasped hands stretched towards heav'n, my eager gaze
Fixed on the widening glory!
     Suddenly,
As if the burden of the flesh no more
Could fetter down the aspiring soul to earth,
As if the fleshly nature were consumed—
Lost in the glowing ecstasy of love—
I soared aloft, I mounted through the air
Free as a spirit, rose to meet my Lord
With such a cry of rapture—that I woke!

Oh! misery, to wake in darkness, wake
From vision of unutterable joy,
Instead of trumpet-sound and song of heaven,
To hear the dull clock measuring out time,
When I had seemed to touch eternity!
In the first pang of disappointed hope,
I wept that I could wake from such a dream.
Until Faith gently whispered, "Wherefore weep
To lose the faint dim shadow of a joy
Of which the substance shall one day be thine?
Live in the hope,—that hope shall brighten life
And sanctify it to its highest end."

Fast roll the chariot wheels of time. HE comes!
The Spirit and the Bride expectant wait,—
Even so come, Lord Jesus! Saviour—come!

www.ingramcontent.com/pod-product-compliance
Lightning Source LLC
Chambersburg PA
CBHW021134020426
42331CB00005B/761